CW01648564

'Get into' Plumbing

'Get into' Plumbing

with Roy Day

This edition produced exclusively for
WHSMITH

ABOUT THE AUTHOR

Trained as an interior designer, Roy Day has spent many years as a writer, broadcaster and television presenter on the various aspects of home improvement. More recently he has diversified into landscape design and produced his first documentary for BBC television. 'A Garden for Chelsea' was based on his own award-winning garden at the Chelsea Flower Show. Roy Day is currently dividing his time between writing the new series of 'Get Into' books and producing more programmes on home interest and arts subjects for video and television. The first four titles in this new mini-book series are *Get into Decorating*, *Get into Carpentry*, *Get into Plumbing* and *Get into Home Electrics*.

ACKNOWLEDGMENTS

The author would like to thank the following for their co-operation in providing photographs: Armitage Shanks Ltd; The Haigh Engineering Company Ltd; Walker Crosweller & Co Ltd; Harvey Softeners Ltd; Barking – Grohe Ltd.

Cover photography by Michael Plomer

This edition produced exclusively for W H Smith

Published by
Deans International Publishing
52-54 Southwark Street, London SE1 1UA
A division of The Hamlyn Publishing Group Limited
London · New York · Sydney · Toronto

Copyright © The Hamlyn Publishing Group Limited 1983
ISBN 0 603 03111 0

All rights reserved. No part of this publication may be reproduced, stored in a retrieval system, or transmitted, in any form or by any means, electronic, mechanical, photocopying, recording or otherwise, without the permission of The Hamlyn Publishing Group Limited.

Printed in Italy

Contents

Introduction

The supply of fresh water to the home and the disposal of dirty water and sewage, is so much part of our daily lives that while these two vital services are running effectively, we take them very much for granted.

Then something goes wrong: it may be a simple blockage that prevents the water running away from the basin, or a slightly loose pipe connection which starts that horrible stain on the ceiling that grows rapidly before your eyes.

Whatever the reason for these problems, there is always an immediate tendency to panic and run to the yellow pages for the help of the nearest available plumber.

So often the remedy is easy to effect with the help of a tool which you may already possess – assuming of course that you already have a little bit of experience of doing basic repairs.

This book is primarily concerned with explaining the principles of water supply and disposal in the home. Once you have grasped this and become familiar with the various components involved, then you will be well on the way to getting into plumbing and pulling the toilet flush will never be quite the same experience again.

A well-appointed bathroom, with sanitary ware in the latest fashionable colour, has become a much admired and sought-after status symbol in the modern home.

The choice of fittings is wide and varied with a

large selection of taps and accessories to appeal to those with the most discerning of tastes.

Properly set out it should provide a room which is both practical and pleasant to be in. But let us not lose sight of the fact that a bathroom cannot function efficiently without adequate plumbing and a constant supply of water.

The Water Supply

Household supplies of domestic water are carried from the water authority reservoirs to all residential areas in iron mains, which are set down under the highways.

Every property receives its individual supply by means of a connection pipe which runs to a water authority stopcock – normally this is set in the pavement and has a hinged lid over it. This stopcock is usually about 1 m/3ft below ground and requires a special turn key to operate it. The end of the turn key slips over a shanked top and the wide handles provide sufficient leverage to turn the supply on and off. This needs to be done very seldom unless the authority inspectors are working on the supply in the road.

Avoid the temptation to let dense vegetation grow over and hide your stopcock cover. Like manhole inspection covers they should be readily accessible at all times in case they are needed in an emergency. Your responsibility for the water supply into your own home starts at the water authority stopcock. From there a service pipe carries it well below ground – for frost protection – through the foundations and into the house. This can be a considerable distance depending on the length of your front garden. Your service pipe could be made of lead or cast iron if the property was built in the earlier part of the century. Most modern dwellings usually have a 15mm/½in copper supply pipe.

It is important that this supply pipe is adequately protected on its journey into the house. Usually it passes through old drain pipes as a safeguard against subsidence or any damage which could occur through garden excavation. Its depth in the ground is usually adequate to ensure protection against frost even in the severest of winters. When your service pipe enters the house under a timber floor, check to see whether it is well protected and lagged against icy draughts because this is a vulnerable area especially if an air vent is situated close to it. It will pay to spend time doing this job well if the builder has neglected it.

It is important that you know where your service pipe comes into the house. Often this is sited in the kitchen but it could be in any other convenient spot close to the front of the property. At a short distance from the floor you will find a stopcock which should have a draincock immediately above. It may be a combined stop-valve and drain cock. This main stopcock is certainly the most important plumbing fitting in the house. Turn it on and off from time to time to see that it is in working order, as it can stick fast if it is left unused for really long periods.

It is the valve which stops the flow of water to the storage tank and it should be turned off if the house is to be left unoccupied for long periods especially

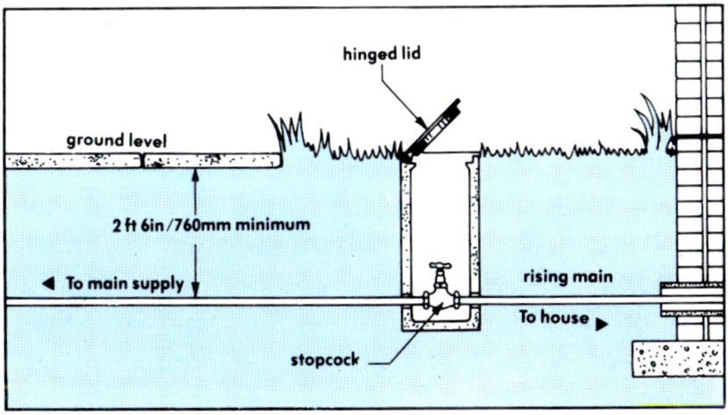

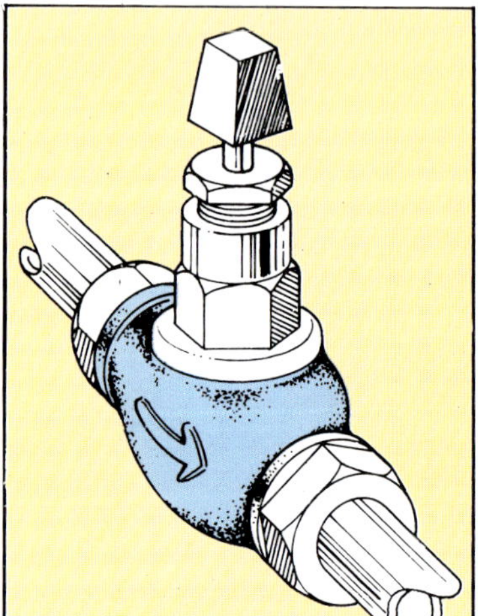

Typical exterior stopcock

in the winter months. If it were left on and a pipe were to split due to intense frost, water would run unabated as soon as the ice had melted.

Remember that with an efficiently operating mains stopcock shut off, you can carry out any type of work to the plumbing in the house in complete safety having first drained away any unwanted water. In an emergency it is the stopcock which controls the flow of water into the house and once this has been closed down you can then attend to the trouble in question. When repairs have to be made to the stopcock itself or to the service pipe immediately preceding it, then you will need to turn off the flow from the outside, at the authority stopcock, to deal with it.

A word here about plumbing materials and the question of metrication in the industry. There is as much confusion in the British Isles as far as the layman is concerned over plumbing components as there is over the various other materials used by the building trade at large. It is a fact of life that metric sizes and the old imperial measurements will run

Interior stop valve

Draincock

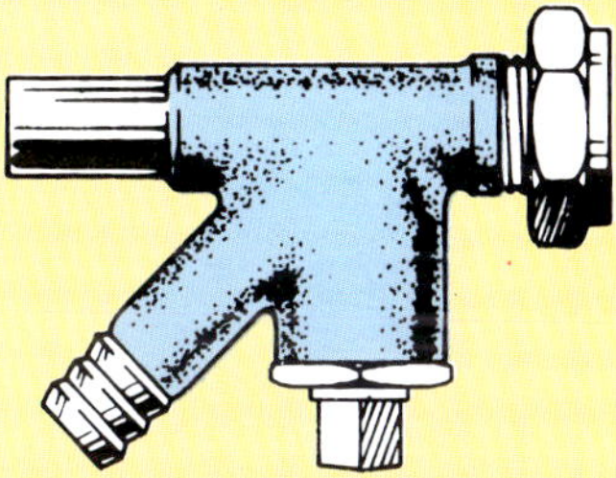

Combined stop valve and draincock

side by side for a considerable time to come. Until the official change to metrication, the most common sizes of copper pipe to be used in the home were ½in, ¾in and 1in and these measurements referred to the internal diameter of the pipe in each instance. Today the equivalent sizes are 15mm, 22mm and 28mm which refer to the external diameter of a thinner walled copper pipe and stainless steel tube.

It is inevitable that this new material will have to be coupled to the existing old pipework in many houses, especially where extensions are being built and there is the need for additional pipework to bathrooms, enlarged kitchen areas and utility rooms. In most cases straight connectors are available but where this is not the case, adaptors and reducers can be used to overcome the problem.

Cold Water Systems

Your main cold water supply or rising main as it is often called has two or three functions to perform. It rises into the loft to supply the cold water storage tank to a consistent level via a ball valve. It supplies the kitchen tap with cold water which provides drinking water, and it may supply an outside tap for the garden or cleaning the car.

Both the kitchen tap and the outside tap are supplied with water from T-junction fittings set into the rising main and it is important that a stop valve is also fitted on the branch feeding the outside tap. Fit one with an arrow marked onto the body of the valve and make sure that it points in the same direction as the flow to the outside. This directional flow fitting is used as a safeguard against polluted water being drawn back into the domestic supply. It is very unlikely to happen but if the rising main stopcock was closed off and the kitchen tap turned on, it might be possible to siphon back dirty water through a hose which had been left in a water butt with the garden tap in the open position.

Cold water storage tank

The cold water storage tank has an important part to play in supplying all the other requirements for water in the house.

The tank is sited at the top of a house over a load-bearing wall usually in the loft. The capacity of the tank may be 225 litres/50 galls and it will weigh over 200kg/4cwt full. The rising main is connected near the top of the tank and a ball valve maintains the required water level.

Just above the water level line another pipe is connected to act as an overflow. This pipe should be 22mm/$\frac{3}{4}$in diameter and is taken in a downward slope to the outside of the house. When water runs from this overflow, it is a warning that the valve requires attention.

Cold water supply points

Two 22mm/$\frac{3}{4}$in pipes run from the bottom of the storage tank, both controlled by gate valves. One pipe supplies the cold water requirements in the bathroom with connections going to all cold water taps and the toilet cistern. The other pipe goes to the bottom of the hot water cylinder to replenish the demand for hot water in the kitchen and bathroom.

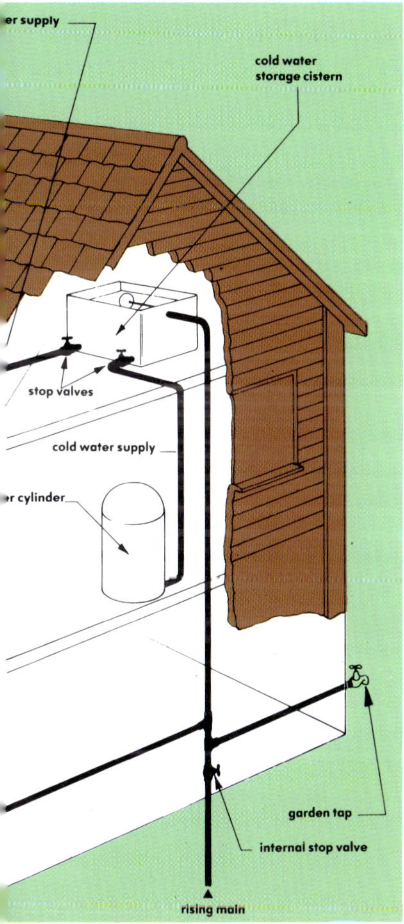

Hot Water Systems

The simplest method of providing hot water is by using an electric immersion heater. The element of the heater is set into the cylinder and switched on to provide hot water when required. A thermostat will control the temperature level for economy.

The hot water is drawn off from the top of the tank and soon after this pipe leaves the cylinder, a T-connection takes a second 22mm/$\frac{3}{4}$in branch pipe which rises up into the loft to hang open ended over the cold water storage tank. This is a vent pipe which has to be installed for safety purposes.

If the thermostat were to fail and the water continue to heat to boiling point, steam would rise and condense back into the storage tank above. This tank continually replenishes the hot water cylinder below with cold water.

Direct hot water system

Your water may be heated by a boiler which is fired with solid fuel, gas or oil. Cold water flows from the bottom of the cylinder, is heated in the boiler and flows back to enter the cylinder at the top. Care must be taken to see that the boiler is not allowed to run flat out when hot water is not being used, causing it to boil in the storage cylinder.

The vent pipe would be the only safety outlet if the taps were not turned on to release the pressure. A drain cock should always be fitted at the lowest point of the boiler flow pipe to enable complete drainage at any time.

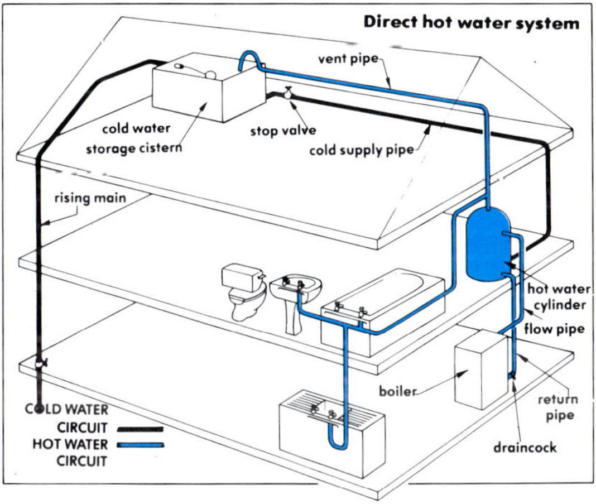

Indirect hot water system

This works on a totally different principle from the direct system using two completely separate water circuits. A different type of hot water cylinder is used, inside which there is a smaller cylinder or calorifier. The primary circuit consists of water flowing continuously in a loop from boiler to calorifier. Unless the system is drained down, the water is used over and over again, topped up from its own header tank. Water in the main cylinder is heated directly and supplied to the taps by passing over this primary circuit. Radiators for central heating can also be supplied by this primary circuit all running off the same boiler.

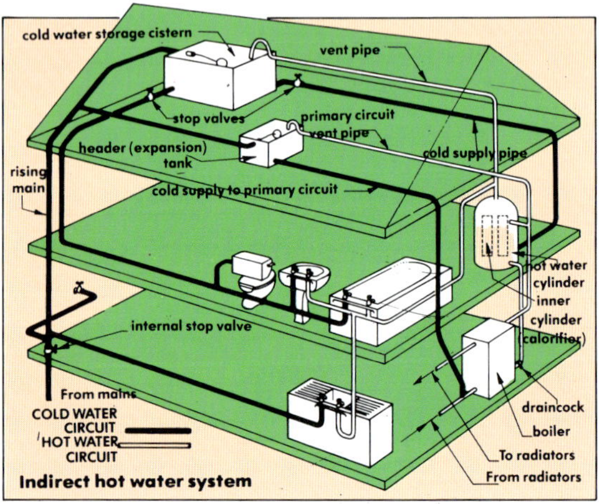

Indirect hot water system

Expansion or header tank

This header tank has an important role to play as far as the primary circuit is concerned. Like the cold water storage tank it is fed from the rising main and the flow into the header tank is controlled by a ball valve. The water level in this tank should be kept low, usually it is only 75mm/3in or 100mm/4in from the bottom. This is to allow for water to expand back up the cold supply pipe of the primary circuit when heated by the boiler which considerably raises the water level in the tank. As it cools it returns back into the circuit. It is very much a second version of the main cold storage tank and like that, it must have a 22mm/$\frac{3}{4}$in outlet pipe to the exterior of the building to act as an overflow. Should the ball valve jam in the open position, water will flow down this pipe and prevent internal flooding.

Frost Precautions and Bursts

Burst pipes account for most of the plumbing catastrophies which occur in the home and for this reason every precaution should be taken to protect the pipework against an excessive fall in temperature below freezing.

A loft area is the most obvious place where trouble is likely to occur, especially if the loft has been well insulated against heat loss from the rooms below. See that everything is lagged thoroughly, especially vulnerable bends, vent pipes and overflows. Also see that tanks are well covered including lids.

A leak can occur in various ways due to frost. A compression joint may spring open due to ice pressure. Usually this is one of the easiest to repair by simply loosening the nut, pushing the pipe back into place and retightening the nut. If the leak is not cured it may be necessary to replace the olive. A sprung soldered joint can be more difficult to repair and certainly all the water will have to be drained out before any heat is applied to the pipe. Often it is easier to cut out the damaged joint and replace it with a new piece of pipe using two compression fittings as you would if the pipe had split open.

Pipes

The great majority of pipework used in domestic plumbing is either 15mm/$\frac{1}{2}$in or 22mm/$\frac{3}{4}$in copper tube. Once you have learned how to cut, join and bend it then you will be well on the way to doing your own plumbing jobs in the home.

Use a small hacksaw to cut pipes, sawing it as squarely as possible and then remove any burrs from both inside and outside edges with a small file. The job is made easier with a tube cutter if a lot of cutting has to be done. This is clamped around the pipe and rotated while gradually increasing the pressure on the cutting blade.

Jointing

When it comes to joining pipe, you have a choice of fittings. Compression joints are certainly the easiest to use although they are the most expensive available.

This type of fitting has a threaded end to each outlet onto which is screwed a large cap nut. Between these is a separate copper collar known as an olive. The cap nut and olive are pushed onto the end of the pipe, which is then pushed into the body of the fitting as far as it will go. This nut should be turned finger tight before giving it one complete turn with a spanner. If the joint seeps when the water is turned on, simply tighten the nut a little more. You will need a couple of adjustable spanners in your tool kit for use with compression fittings. The jaws should open up to about

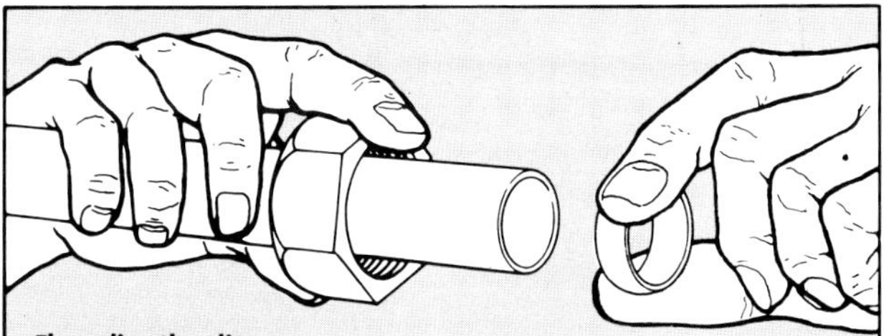

Threading the olive

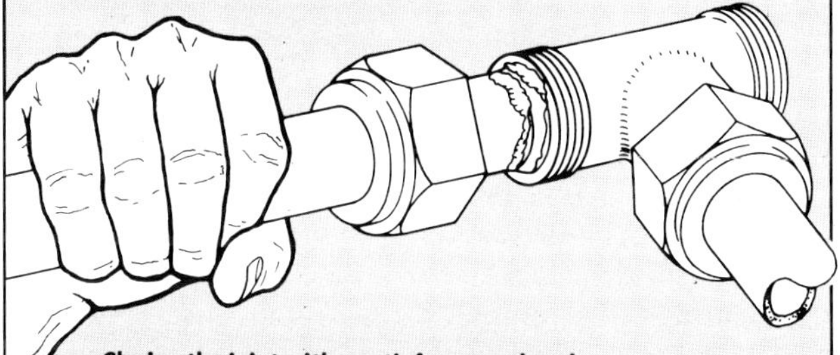

Closing the joint with mastic for a good seal

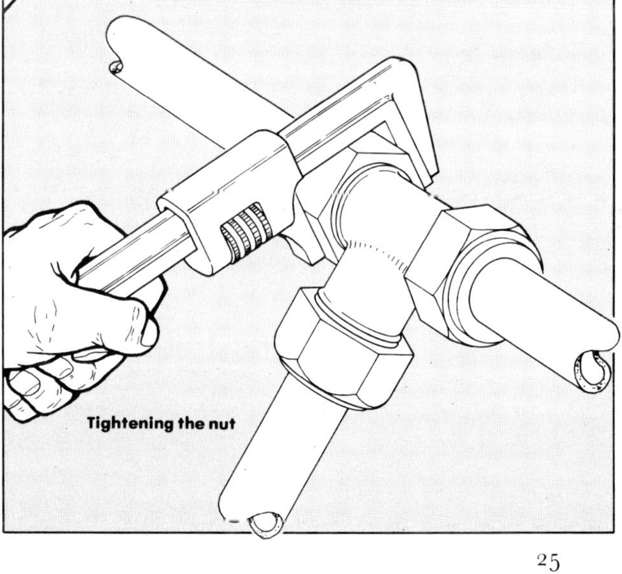

Tightening the nut

35mm/1⅜in as this will cope with most of the fittings you are likely to use. Valves, tees, elbows and reducers can all be used in this way and the advantage of this type of joint is that it can be taken apart as quickly as it is put together.

Capillary joints

These are far less expensive than compression joints but they have to be soldered together. To do this the outside of the pipe is cleaned with wire wool and smeared with flux before being pushed into the fitting. The joint is then heated with a blowtorch until it is hot enough to melt the solder when brought into contact with it. The molten solder will flood between the two surfaces to form a perfect seal when it cools.

There are capillary fittings available which are slightly more expensive which have a ring of solder already placed inside the neck, these are known as Yorkshire fittings. After applying flux in the same way as for the end feed type, heating with a blowtorch is all that is required to complete the joint. Capillary fittings are less bulky than compression joints and they can be taken apart by reheating, but any water will have to be drained away first. **Warning** When using a blowtorch see that a fire-resistant matt is placed behind the heat point to prevent surrounding damage. These matts are available from plumbers' merchants.

Bending Pipes

Forming curves in copper pipe requires special equipment if the shape of the section is to remain undistorted. A bending spring is useful for the smaller diameter pipework. Make sure that you use the right spring for the tube and grease it before inserting it.

The pipe can be bent over the knee quite easily. Slightly over bend it then bring it back to the required curve as this will make the retrieving of the spring easier. It helps to put a bar through the loop in the end and then turn in a clockwise direction as you withdraw it. It is useful to have a small bending machine if a lot of pipe has to be bent, especially if working with 22mm/¾in pipe.

A light-weight bending machine has two separate formers supplied with it for both 15mm/½in and 22mm/¾in pipes. This is a useful tool for bending 15mm/½in stainless steel tube which is a harder material to work with than copper.

Black polythene tube is often used for cold water supply to outside taps where it can be buried underground. Joints are made with compression fittings and bends can be formed by softening the tube in really hot water for a while. Unsupported it is inclined to sag.

Ball Valves

You may have three or four different types of ball valve in the house and it is essential that they all work efficiently, as they control the water level in the storage tanks and cisterns.

Two problems can arise from faulty ball valves, the valve can stick shut preventing the flow of water into the tank or it can jam open causing the water to run continually through the overflow pipe. The Portsmouth valve was the most common valve used and is very likely to jam up particularly in hard water areas where scale builds up around the piston. Inside the piston there is a washer which may need replacing, as one which is damaged prevents the valve from functioning properly.

To inspect it, turn off the water supply to the cistern and remove the split pin holding the float arm in position. Unscrew the end cap and take out the piston which can then be taken apart to renew the washer. Lightly grease the piston with vaseline before putting it back.

The Croydon valve was also used a lot and had a piston with a vertical action, which was rather noisy to operate. Continuing trouble with either type indicates that you should change to a more modern valve.

Every valve is operated by means of a float which is situated at the end of an arm. It rises and falls with the water level causing the valve to open and close. On some arms the float can be adjusted to the required position.

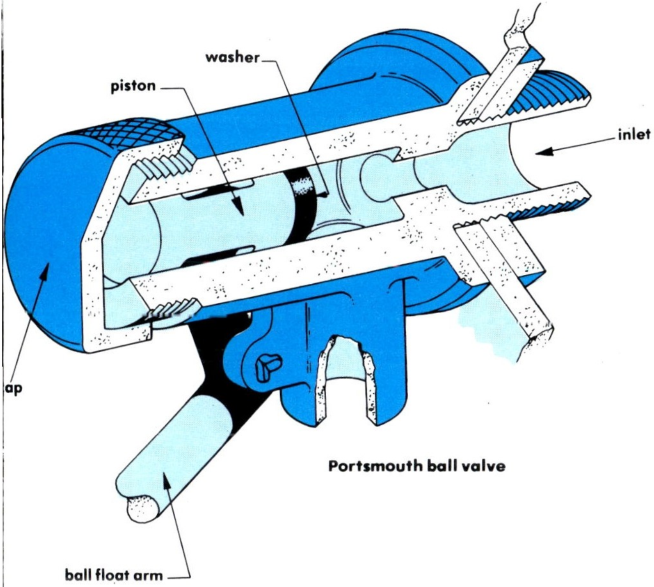

Portsmouth ball valve

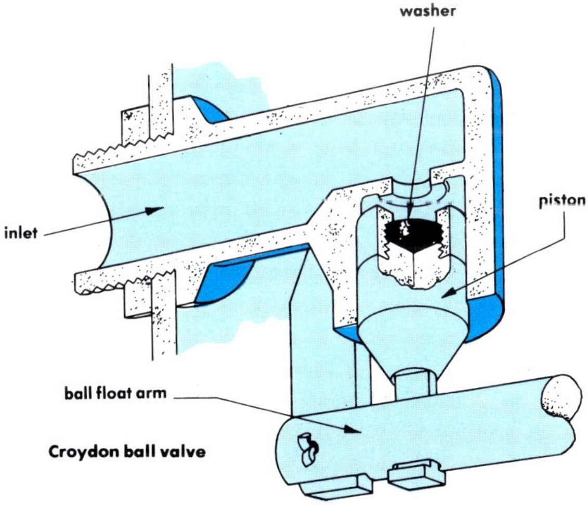

Croydon ball valve

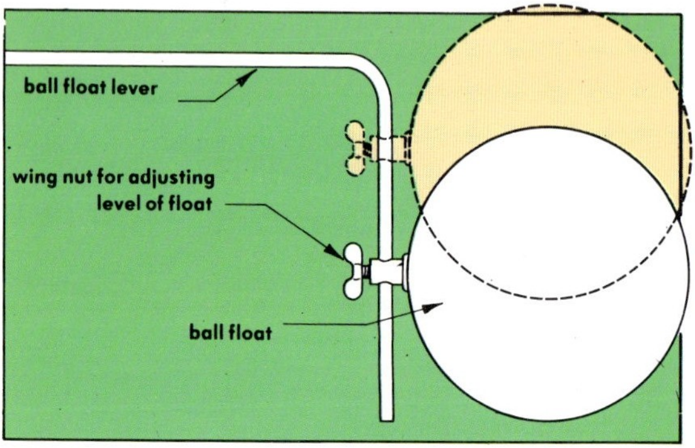

Occasionally a float becomes perforated and fills with water so it needs to be replaced unless you decide to change the complete valve assembly. A diaphragm valve is far less likely to be affected by corrosion. The flow of water is controlled by a rubber diaphragm closing onto a nylon nozzle as the float arm rises with the water. A knurled cap can be unscrewed to remove the diaphragm for cleaning if any dirt gets trapped behind it. The action is quiet with overhead outlet jets directed against the inner sides of the cistern. Versions are available to suit low and high water pressure. Other more sophisticated valves are used to combat variation in mains pressure like the Equilibrium and Torbeck valves. It is worth installing one of these if you are troubled with water hammer, a banging which occurs when a cistern refills due to the rapid opening and closing of the valve.

Taps

Apart from ball valves in cisterns all other outlets for your water supply in the home are controlled by taps.

The first sign that something is going wrong with a tap is when it will not shut off completely and continues to drip. This usually means that a new washer is required. Changing a washer is a job which every householder should be able to do but there are one or two problems which might have to be overcome in the process. Always see that the water supply to the tap is turned off first, unless it is a Supatap which we will consider later.

To expose the headgear of a tap the cover will first have to be removed which may entail taking off the handle. This is usually held in place by a screw which might be concealed under lift-out hot and cold labels. Hard water scale can often seal detachable parts together and a certain amount of force will be required to separate them. Take care how you go about applying force as the chrome finish can be easily scratched and ruined. The jaws of a wrench should be well padded and a thin piece of wood placed under a handle when tapping it away from the spindle.

To unscrew a stubborn easyclean cover, tack a strip of leather to a small length of wood and wrap the leather in an anti-clockwise direction around the cover. The wood acts as a tourniquet as it tightens the leather to loosen the joint. A slim-jawed wrench can then be inserted to grip the nut

Unscrewing an easyclean cover

at the top of the headgear. It may be necessary to support the body of the tap with another padded wrench before you start to unscrew the headgear.

Once the headgear is removed you will discover whether the combined jumper and washer is pegged into it, or drops out as a separate component. Either way the nut at the end will have to be undone to release the old washer. The alternative is to fit a new combined jumper and washer.

It is useful to keep a few spare washers in the house to fit the various sizes of tap on bath and basin. Before putting the tap together again do make sure that the seating in the bottom of the tap body is clean. Any scale or grit present can prevent the new washer closing down tightly and then the tap will continue to drip. A badly pitted seating can be cleaned back with a seating tool but this is an expensive item and you would be better advised

Removing head gear

to use a new nylon washer and seating kit instead as a remedy. The flanged nylon seating is pushed into the existing brass seating of the tap. There is a push-on washer that fits the jumper giving a perfect seal when the two parts of the kit are closed together.

Supataps

These can be rewashered without having to turn off the water supply to them. The retaining nut can be unscrewed and the nozzle removed – the water will stop running when the check valve drops inside the body of the tap. A new washer and jumper can then be inserted and the tap re-assembled.

Mixer taps

These are popular in bathrooms and kitchens but there are regulations concerning their design. The hot and cold water in bathroom fittings can be

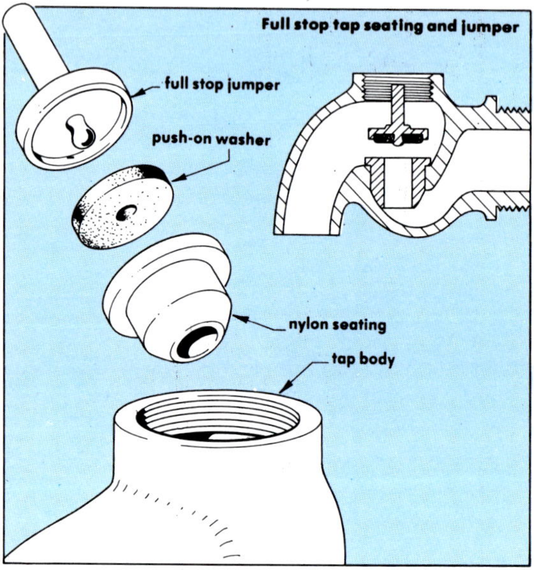

mixed in the body of the tap as both sources are drawn from the storage tank. Where main water is used in kitchen fittings the mixing with the storage hot supply must take place outside the body of the tap. The water authorities insist on this to safeguard against the possibility of contaminated water being drawn back into the main supply.

Generally speaking taps divide into two main categories. The Bib tap has a horizontal inlet and is usually wall mounted, whereas the Pillar tap has a vertical inlet rising through a bath, basin or sink unit.

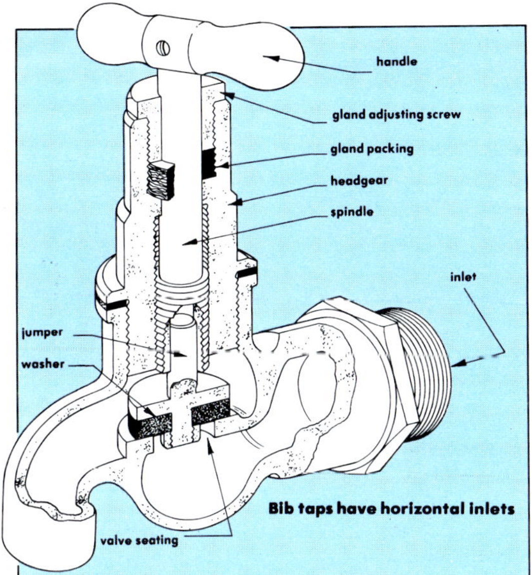

Bib taps have horizontal inlets

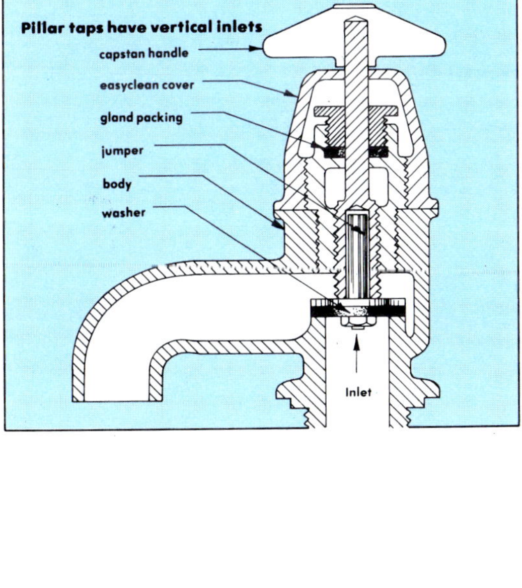

Pillar taps have vertical inlets

Drainage and Disposal of Water

There have been considerable changes in the way that plumbing waste is drained from a building. Most of these developments came about during the mid-1960s. A 2-pipe system was used until that time, which is clearly evident today in the form of cast-iron pipes attached to the outside of buildings.

The soil pipe is the larger diameter pipe to which the one or more WCs are attached. This runs directly underground to be connected to the sewer at one end and rises to a height of 60cm or 90cm/2 or 3 feet above the roof line at the other, where it is left open ended as a vent pipe. It is a common practice to fit a stout cage onto the top of the vent pipe as a precaution against birds nesting there, which could lead to a blockage.

The other main pipe in this system discharges the waste from baths and basins into an open gully at ground level. Usually the wastes on the first floor level discharge into a hopper set at the top of the main pipe and the ground floor kitchen waste runs in a separate pipe to the same gully. Frequently the waste outlets from numerous rooms come together to break up the design of an elevation.

Single stack drainage uses one main pipe inside the house to serve all WCs and water outlets. This runs straight underground into the main sewer and is vented at the other end above the roof line. Cast iron has given way to PVC plastic pipe in the majority of constructions and joints are formed with solvent welds.

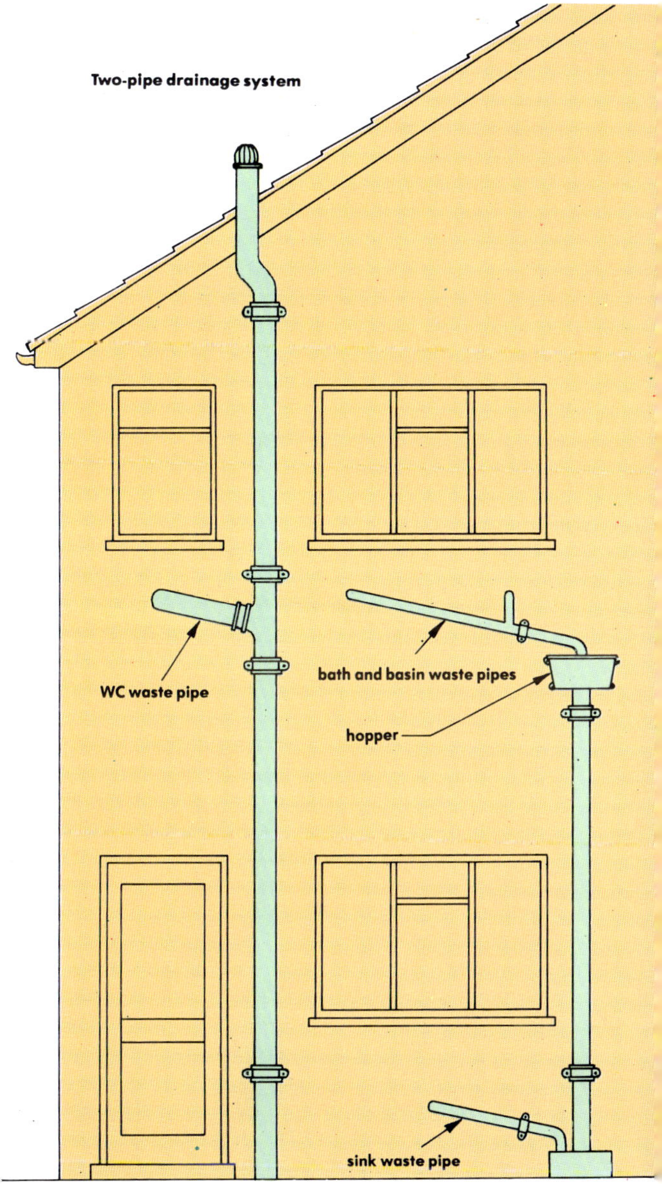
Two-pipe drainage system
WC waste pipe
bath and basin waste pipes
hopper
sink waste pipe

Blockages to waste pipes

These are most likely to occur in the trap, which is a pocket of water that remains beneath a bath, basin or sink. It acts as a barrier against smells rising back from the sewer and entering the house.

In older installations, the trap is likely to be a metal fitting with a small plug screwed into the bottom. When this is blocked the screw can be removed and the debris hooked out into a bucket using a piece of wire as a probe. A modern plastic trap is much easier to deal with. It can be completely disconnected and flushed through if it is a bottle trap. Before re-assembling a plastic trap check the washers, they may require replacing. If after cleaning the trap the blockage persists, it may be confined to a bend or elbow in the waste pipe, or the outlet to the gully may be blocked outside.

A suction cup is a useful gadget and can often clear a blockage in a trap or pipe. Leave a little water in the basin and block the overflow outlet so that air cannot get into the system – a ball of wet

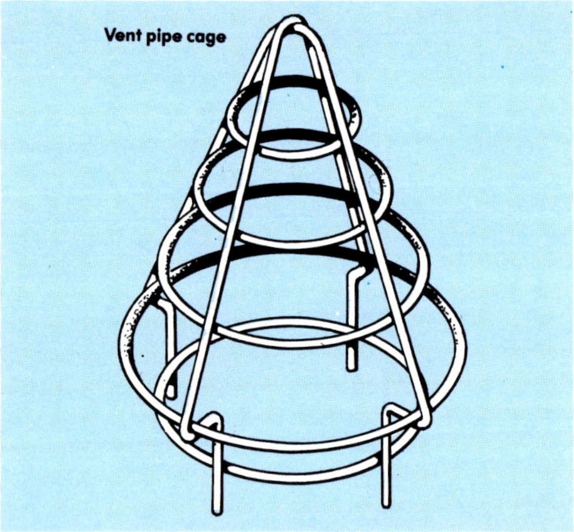

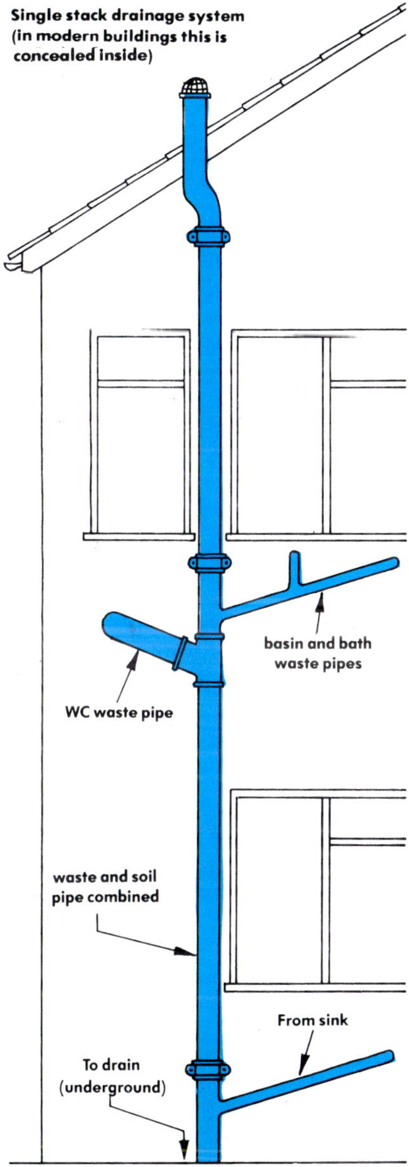
Single stack drainage system
(in modern buildings this is
concealed inside)
basin and bath
waste pipes
WC waste pipe
waste and soil
pipe combined
From sink
To drain
(underground)

rag can be placed over the aperture to block it off. Remember that often the bath and basin connect to the same waste, so both outlets will have to be covered when working on either waste. A few rapid plunge actions with a suction cup over the open waste will often dislodge the debris and draw some back into the basin.

Soap can be a menace and build up over a period of time in a waste pipe, particularly if the fall or downward slope of the pipe is not very great. Check to see if your waste pipe runs horizontally for any distance before turning out through the wall. If it does it may pay you to lower the outlet position to provide a greater fall for the pipe. A soap gel can be broken up with strong boiling soda water. Try this two or three times with household soda and the gel should dissolve away, especially if used with a suction cup. When it clears you should find the slimey evidence deposited in the gully. Thoroughly flush the pipe and gully to complete the job.

Toilet pan blockages

These cause the water to rise dangerously up to the rim when the cistern is flushed. This is often the result of an excessive amount of paper being deposited in the pan – children are sometimes over zealous when it comes to feeding paper down the toilet. To clear it successfully, usually calls for a gloved hand to extract as much of the paper as possible from the bend in the trap.

There are two types of trap. The S-trap is used when connection to the soil pipe or sewer outlet is to be taken down through the floor – usually at ground floor level. The P-trap pan is used when connection is to be made through an outside wall or to an internally ducted soil pipe which is usually at first floor level.

If the blockage persists and cannot be cleared by hand, check the first outside inspection chamber for the cause.

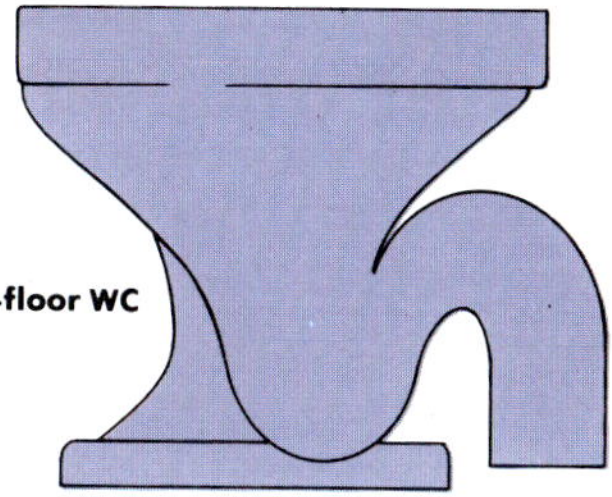

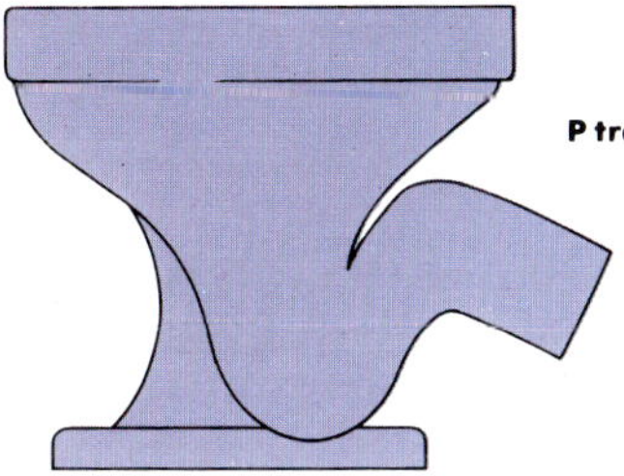

Cistern problems

Poor cistern flushing with a low-level suite usually means that the diaphragm needs replacing. The supply to the cistern must be shut off or the ball valve tied up to a piece of wood. Then when the cistern has been flushed, any remaining water can be bailed out. Release the flushing lever,and the large nut under the cistern and lift out the plastic siphoning mechanism – the damaged diaphragm will then be clearly visible. Replacements can be obtained from plumbers' merchants or can be cut to the exact diameter from a suitable piece of plastic. Once the fittings have been re-assembled, the water can be turned on and the problem should be cured.

Close coupled siphonic WCs are the latest development in lavatory pans dispensing with the need for a flush pipe. These work with a siphonic action where the level of water in the pan drops before the flushing water arrives to replace it.

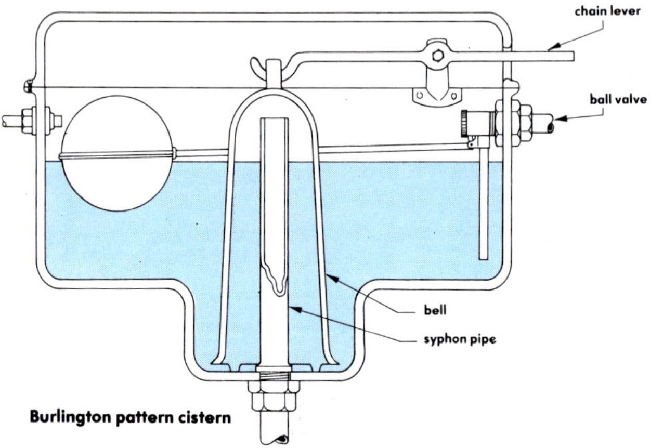

Burlington pattern cistern

Reference should be made here to the old high-level Burlington pattern cisterns which are now rapidly becoming antiques. These work by siphonic action, when a bell is raised by pulling a chain. Water is drawn up over the siphon pipe causing a partial vacuum which is only broken when air gets under the bell. Grit or corrosion can get under the bell and should be cleaned out.

Another problem which can occur is when the water flows into the cistern too rapidly causing the water to run continually when flushed. This can be cured by closing down the stop valve to restrict the flow of water from the storage tank to the cistern.

Although noisy, these old-fashioned, high-level cisterns seldom give trouble. When problems arise it usually means that a change should be considered to a modern low-level suite.

Outside drains

The final stage of sewage and water disposal from the house is through the drains themselves. These were formed from salt glazed pipe in older constructions and have been largely superseded in modern house development with pitch fibre or plastic pipes.

Various drainage pipes come together in one main pipe which steadily slopes down to join the main sewer in the road. Manholes are placed at strategic points where junctions occur and form access points for rodding through to a blockage. If a manhole fills with water this indicates that the blockage is on the main sewer side of that inspection chamber. The first most likely place for a blockage to occur is at an outside gully and there could be one of two reasons for this. The most common cause is leaves and debris blocking the grid covering the gully. In no time at all waste water from the bathroom and kitchen will flood the surrounding paths. A gully grid should be cleaned at regular intervals, especially in the late autumn when leaves are blown about. A badly clogged iron grid can be placed in an open fire and burnt clean. When it cools it should be thoroughly wire brushed and painted before being put back into the gully.

In the bottom of the gully there is a water seal which is similar to a trap in a WC. This prevents gases escaping back from the sewer. It can silt up with sand or congealed soap as well as any leaves and debris which may have got beneath the grid cover. If this has happened it will form a blockage and cause overflow problems. The fault can be checked by lifting the first inspection cover. This should be clear of any build up of water, confirming that the problem lies in the gully itself. Clean out the trap thoroughly, removing as much of the debris as possible with a gloved hand. Then flush it through with a running hose to ensure a clean passage.

Make regular checks on these outside trouble areas and this will help to safeguard the smooth running of your waste disposal from bathroom fittings and basins inside the house. Let us now consider a blockage in the main drain.

If you are to try to clear it yourself, a set of cane rods with accessories is essential. These can be

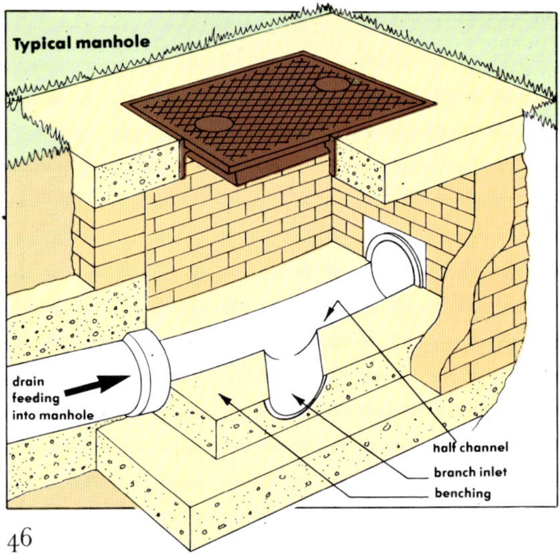
Typical manhole
drain
feeding
into manhole
half channel
branch inlet
benching

hired and are assembled in the same way that a chimney sweep puts his flue rods together.

As the threaded ends of each rod are joined they must be twisted in a clockwise direction whether pushing them into a drain or pulling them out. This will avoid the possibility of their coming apart in the drain below ground which would be disastrous.

The plunger head is ideal for moving soft material forward along the pipe but if a densely tangled obstruction is encountered it may be necessary to fit the corkscrew head to break through it.

A drain blockage due to the penetration of tree roots will not be cleared by rodding and may entail fairly drastic remedial measures such as digging up and replacing an entire section of drain.

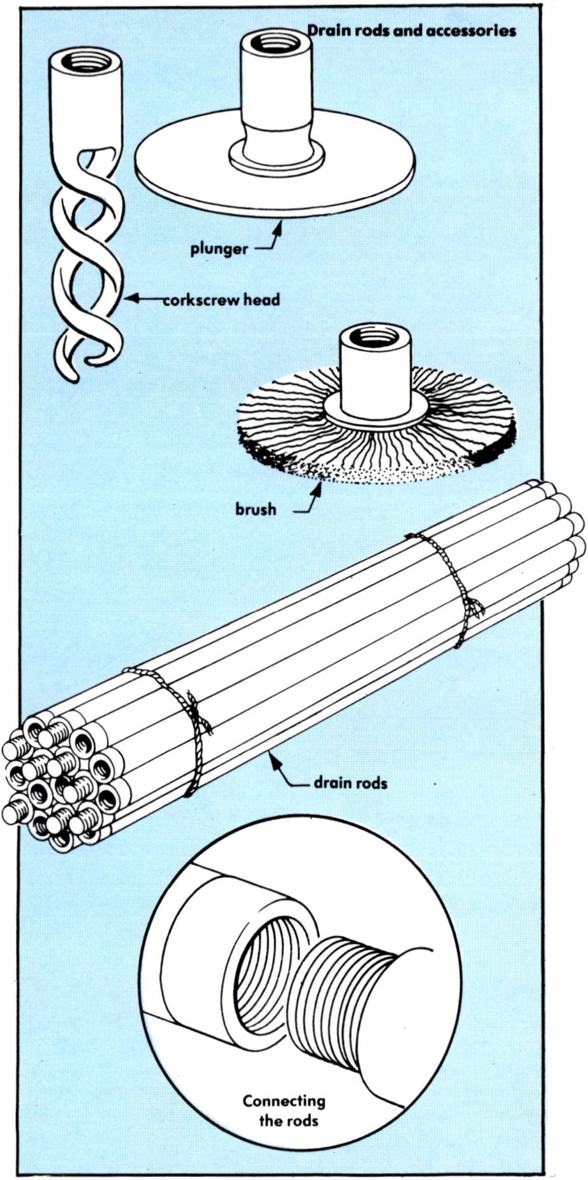
Drain rods and accessories
plunger
corkscrew head
brush
drain rods
Connecting the rods

Rainwater Systems

Incorrectly assembled and poorly maintained gutters and downpipes can cause a great deal of harm to the fabric of a building, certainly as far as penetrating damp is concerned.

However you must be careful when working from a ladder. Always see that it is securely attached to a ring bolt at the top and never lean it against a plastic gutter or even a metal one which is anything less than sturdy.

Make a practice of cleaning out guttering at least once a year as a build up of leaves can lead to overflow problems.

Ladder secured to a ring bolt screwed to a fascia

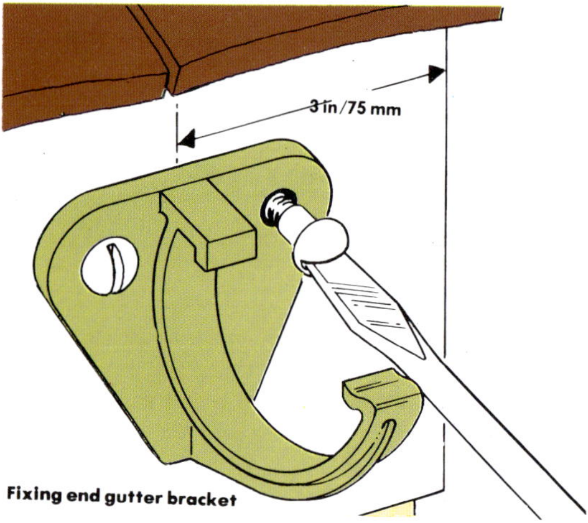

Fixing end gutter bracket

The greatest care should always be taken to see that the guttering is aligned correctly. A run should slope down to the outlet by 12-25mm in 3m/$\frac{1}{2}$in-1in in 10ft. Often carelessness in the assembly stages means that guttering sags before reaching the outlet causing problems. This can be corrected by re-positioning an offending bracket to raise a section of the guttering. Sometimes it may be necessary to dismantle the gutter section to get at the bracket in question.

Brackets can be fascia mounted or fixed to the sides or tops of roof rafters. In older properties the gutter sections could be half round, square or ogee in section with appropriate brackets for each.

Occasionally the mastic seal between sections of cast iron guttering can break down and it will then

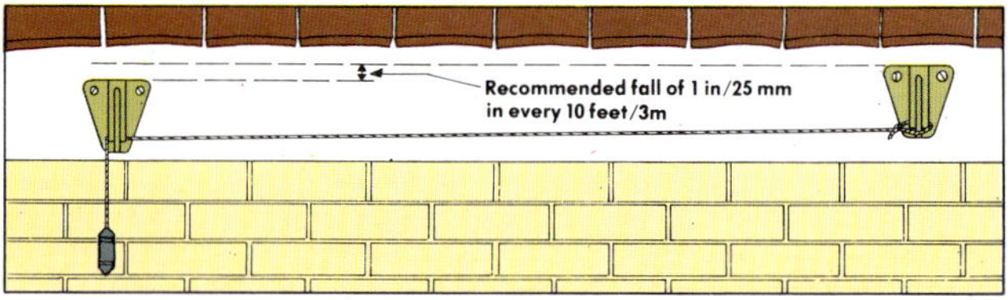

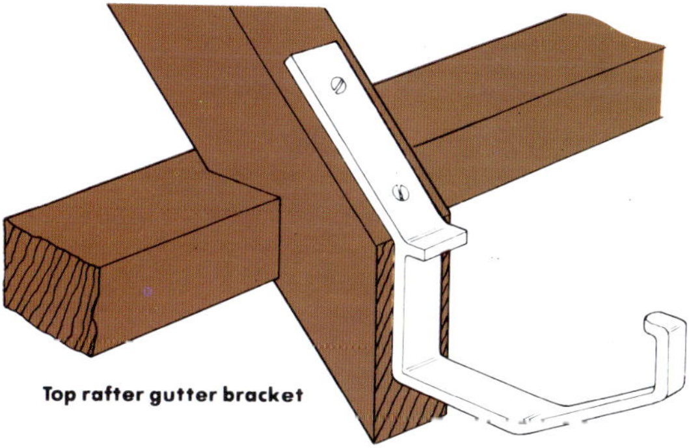

Top rafter gutter bracket

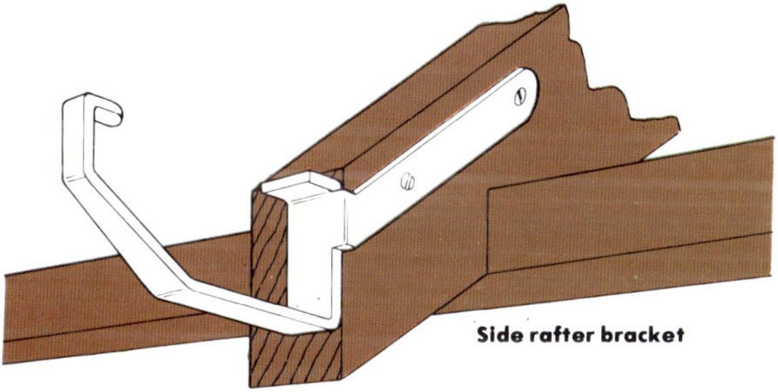

Side rafter bracket

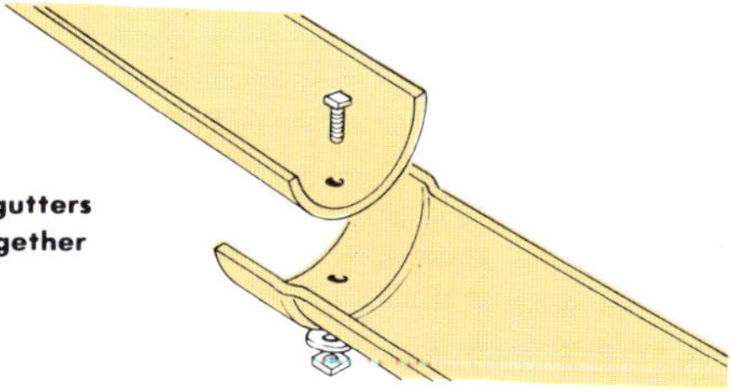

Cast iron gutters
bolted together

be necessary to take the sections apart. It is unlikely that you will be able to undo the nut and bolt at each end as these will be badly corroded. Use a junior hacksaw to cut through them as replacements are easily obtained from builders' merchants. Thoroughly clean away the old putty and any rust scale and then prime the surfaces with a metal primer. Assemble the joint on a new bed of metal casement putty and securely tighten the nut and bolt. Any surplus mastic can then be trimmed

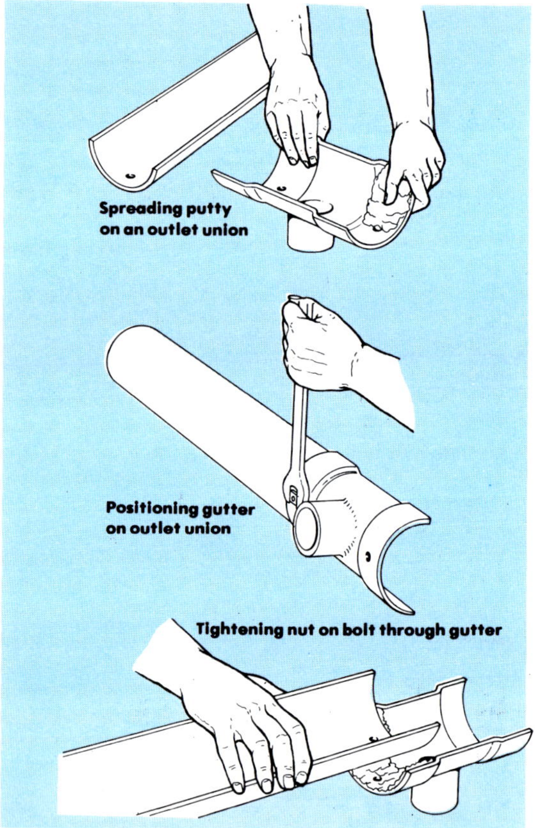

away and both internal and external surfaces given a couple of coats of gloss paint for protection.

Split pipes and gutters can be caused by water freezing over blockages. If a really bad fracture has occurred there will be no alternative but to replace the section in question.

Small repairs can always be made with a glass fibre repair kit of the type used on car bodywork which can then be painted. As soon as you find that the maintenance on metal guttering is becoming too demanding, it is time to change to a plastic system which will not require any painting.

There are several different systems available, each with its own particular method of assembly. The half round section is the most popular and is stocked by DIY stores and plumbers' merchants.

Main components of gutter system

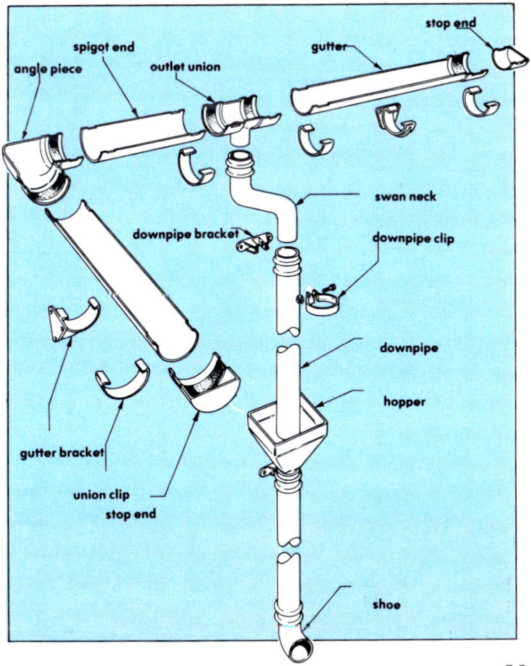

Fitting an Outside Tap

Before fitting an outside tap your local water authority should be informed about this additional supply for a hose before the work is actually done.

It is unlikely that any objection will be raised but your annual water rate will probably be increased to cover the cost of the extra water consumed. It is the normal practice to run an outside tap from the rising main and usually the most difficult part of the job is making a hole through the wall to house the branch pipe. Ideally a hole should be drilled about 25mm/1in in diameter using a long reach masonry drill. These are expensive to purchase and barely worth hiring for one hole, so you may have to resort to the more laborious job of cutting through with a cold chisel and club hammer from either side of the external wall, then make good with sand and cement when the pipe is fitted.

To make the connection, turn off the water at the main stopcock then turn on the kitchen tap to drain the pipe. At the appropriate point, cut out a sufficient length off the pipe with a junior hacksaw to accommodate a tee junction compression fitting. See that the sawn ends are square and free of burrs. When the tee junction has been fitted, fit a stopcock mid-way between the tee junction and the exit position. When this is securely in place the water can be turned on again and the kitchen tap turned off.

Use a compression elbow each side of the wall with a length of 15mm/½in pipe between, which

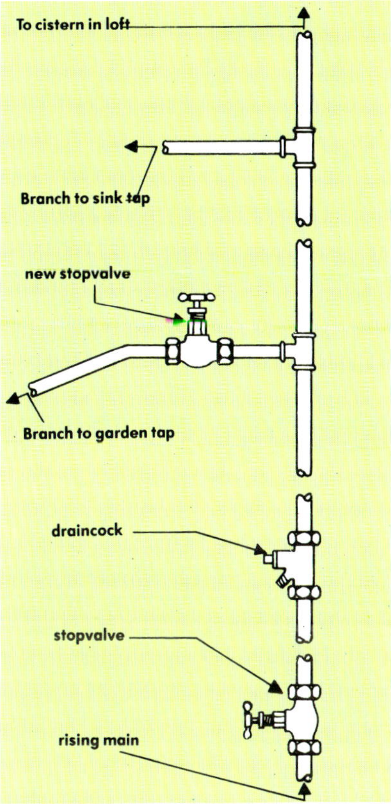

will save having to bend any pipe. The outside tap can be mounted on a wall plate elbow to provide a permanent secure fixing. During the winter months see that the stopcock to the outside tap is turned off and the outside tap itself is turned on. This will prevent icing up during periods of frost.

Extension to an outside tap

Should you want to install a second garden tap as a wall fixing or a stand pipe, this can be done by using a wall plate tee instead of a wall plate elbow to fix the first tap.

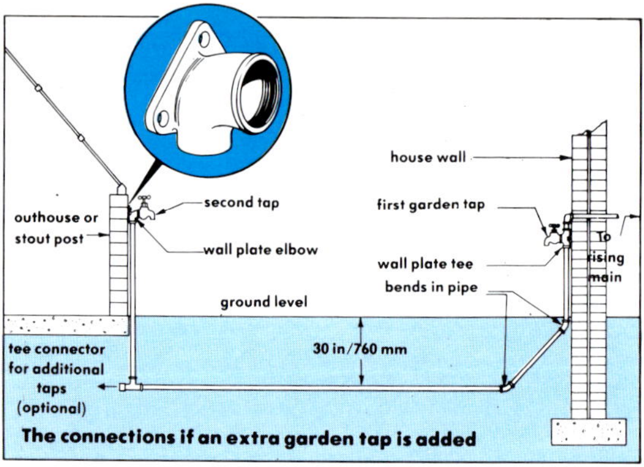

The connections if an extra garden tap is added

Polythene tube can be used with the appropriate compression fittings for any pipe to be buried underground, and this should be set at a depth of about 760mm/30in.

If a garden tap develops a drip when it is turned off, remove the headgear with a spanner and check the washer or look to see if there are any filings or other deposits in the bottom. The seepage may be coming from the gland nut at the top. This can only be tightened so far before the capstan handle becomes difficult to turn. If the water continues to appear it usually indicates that the gland packing needs replacing.

First you will have to unscrew the gland nut and rake out all the old packing with a thin screwdriver blade. It may be necessary to take off the capstan handle first to remove the gland nut and fibre washer. Fresh packing can be made from wool or hemp smeared with vaseline and pressed well into the cavity.

When the tap is re-assembled, tighten the gland nut just enough to provide a watertight seal. Various connectors are available for joining hose pipes to outside taps and these are usually well displayed at established garden centres. A tight fitting is essential to resist back pressure.

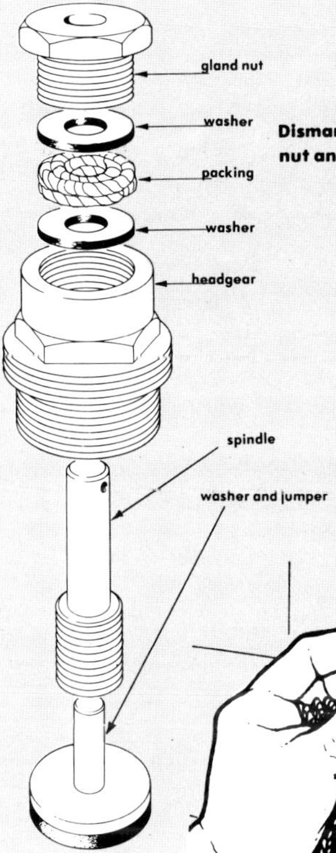

Dismantled tap showing gland nut and other parts

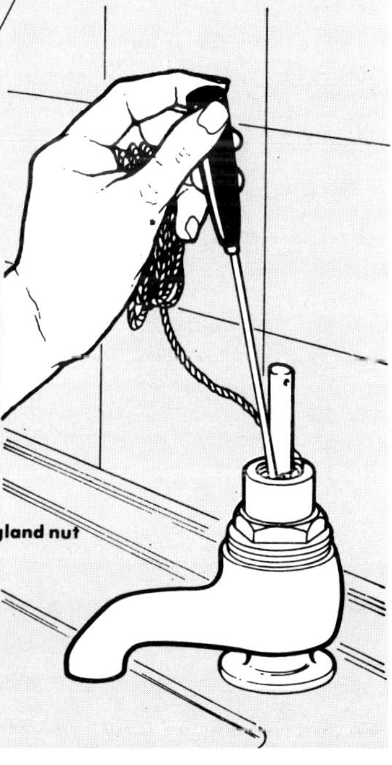

Repacking a gland nut

Replacing a WC Pan

If an existing pan develops a crack it should be changed as it would be unhygienic to leave it in that condition.

The cistern should be completely emptied of water and then the flush pipe can be disconnected by releasing the nut under the cistern and rolling back the rubber cone connector at the back of the pan. If this pipe is cemented into the pan, it will either have to be sawn through or released by breaking the pan away from it with a hammer.

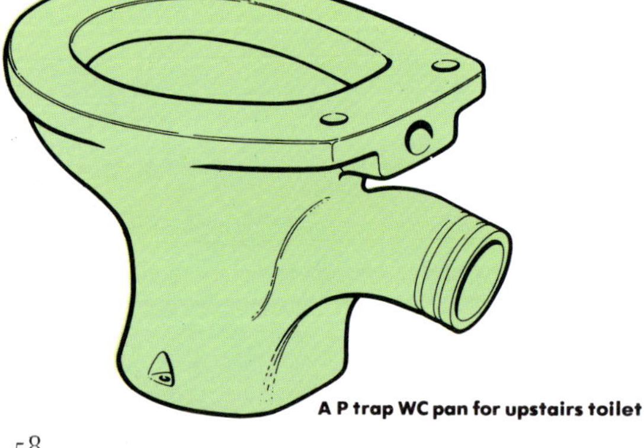

A P trap WC pan for upstairs toilet

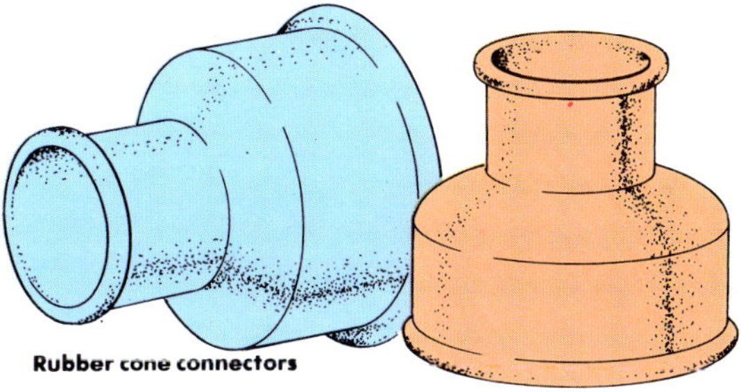

Rubber cone connectors

After bailing out water from the trap the pan can then be removed. Whether it is a P-trap or S-trap pan, if the connection has been made with a cement joint, this will have to be broken away with a club hammer. Take the greatest care that none of the debris enters the drain outlet, as a precaution stuff an old rag into it to seal it off temporarily while you work. Also wear some eye protection and a pair of stout gloves to protect your hands.

When replacing a P-trap pan check that it is level before making it secure to the floor. The position may have to be slightly changed if a new cistern is being installed at the same time. A flexible Multikwik connector can be used to provide the new connection to the soil pipe. Different patterns of these push-on connectors are available to accomodate any change in pipe alignment. It may be possible to use the old flush pipe when the pan is secured, alternatively it may be necessary to fit a new one.

Replacing an S-trap pan on the ground floor is very similar but even more care must be taken when cleaning out the neck of the drain socket to prevent debris falling into the opening. The connection should be made as quickly as possible to prevent smells from the sewer penetrating the house. A push-on drain connector can be used or a quick-drying cement joint can be made instead. If cement is used, place the end of the trap into the

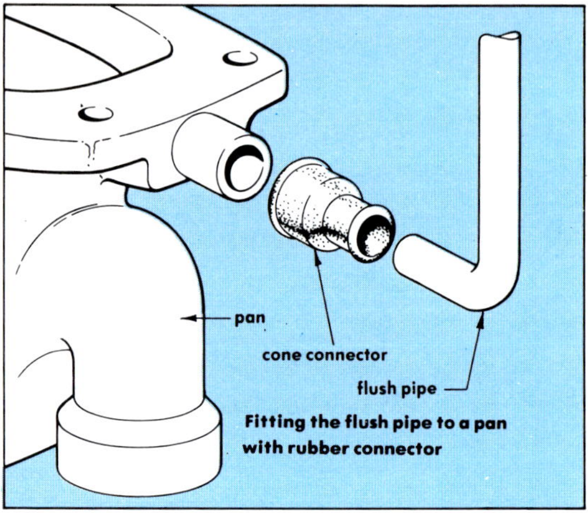

Fitting the flush pipe to a pan with rubber connector

Multi-kwik connectors

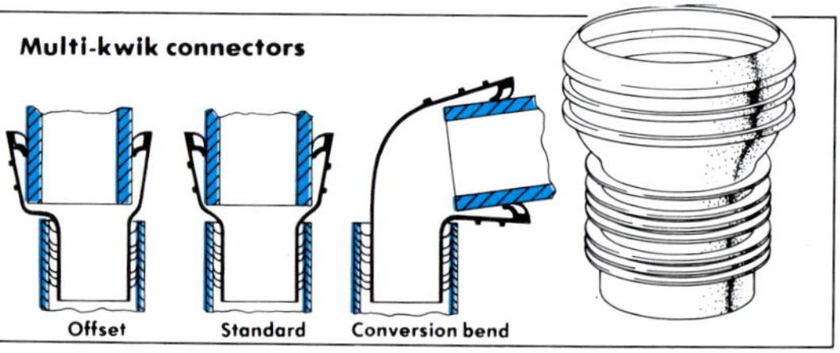

cleaned drain socket, then force some damp newspaper around the perimeter of the joint, packing it well in. This will prevent the cement falling through when it is applied with a trowel to complete the seal. The pan is secured to the floor with brash screws and rubber washers and set into fresh cement on a solid floor.

It may be necessary to replace the toilet seat when you install a new pan, or simply to give an old but otherwise perfect pan a new look. The fixing holes in the top of a pan will accommodate a whole range of different seat patterns which are held in place by finger-tight wing nuts. Modern designs enable the seat and lid to be taken apart quickly for thorough cleaning.

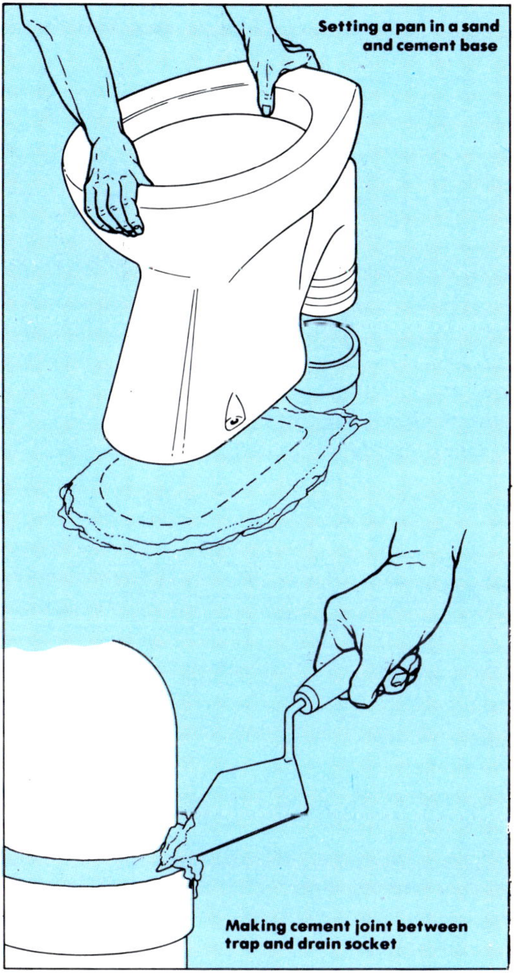
Setting a pan in a sand and cement base
Making cement joint between trap and drain socket

Sink Units

A typical modern floor standing sink unit is anchored into place by the plumbing which passes through the worktop. This means that dirt and dust can collect behind and beneath the unit and prove difficult to remove.

One way to overcome this is to incorporate the hot and cold supply into a rear fascia which is clear of the unit top. In this way the only disconnection required to release the unit would be the unscrewing of the plastic waste trap so that it can be moved forward away from the wall. Alternatively a sink top could be cantilevered, leaving an open space beneath.

Reference has already been made to kitchen mixer taps and these are available with long reach outlets so that the mixer body can be set onto the sill at the rear of the sink top. When the unit is moved forward the plumbing remains fully functional.

The traditional stainless steel sink top pre-drilled for tap connection has found competition in recent years with a range of other surface finishes. These include laminated plastic and ceramic tile which are often used as vanity unit work surfaces into which stainless steel and porcelain or enamelled sinks are set complete with many new types of fittings.

Hand Basins

The plumbing arrangement for a wash basin is very similar to that employed for a kitchen sink. A waste outlet complete with trap drains the water away and hot and cold supply pipes run to the respective taps – the only difference is that the cold supply is drawn from the storage tank and not the mains.

Three different types of basin are widely used. One is wall hung from stout support brackets, the other two are floor supported, either by means of a pedestal or a vanity unit top with storage below. The connections under basins are notoriously difficult to get at and often stubborn to move. If the existing taps are connected by lead pipe, then this should be replaced with new copper pipework. The appearance of an old basin in good condition can often be considerably enhanced by fitting new taps to it.

Once the water supply has been turned off, the coupling nuts can be undone to release the pipework to each tap. The backnuts holding the taps in place will require a special crow's foot spanner to turn them. At this stage great care must be taken to support the tap and this calls for an extra pair of hands. Without support the basin itself can be damaged. Once the old taps have been removed, check the length of the threaded tail against the new ones. Any difference will have to be adjusted on the length of supply pipe before recoupling is carried out.

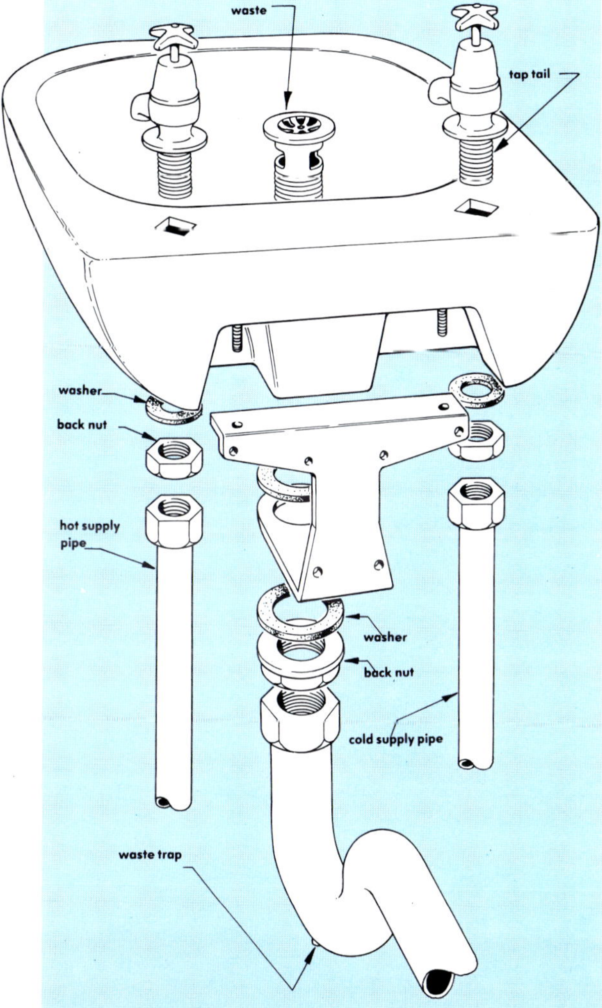

Typical plumbing arrangement of a hand basin

Fitting a New Bath

Removal of a bath panel will often reveal a sordid collection of old milk bottles, cigarette packets and other junk which has long become the haunt for spiders and other insects. Removing the bath will provide an opportunity to clean up this nasty area and make it more hygienic.

First pull away the bath panel and any framing behind it to give greater access to the plumbing, then disconnect all the fittings following the same procedure as for the basin. The larger size of crow's foot spanner will be needed for the backnuts on the bath taps and you may even require a Stilson

wrench on the bath overflow nut.

If the pipework is lead you will need to replace this with new pipework. If copper already exists, take care with this as you will not want to disturb it more than you have to.

Special compression plugs can be fitted to the ends of the supply pipes if the plumbing is to be dismantled for a long period. This will enable the supply to the wash basin and cistern to be used.

The older type cast iron bath is a heavy brute to move, which no doubt accounts for the increasing popularity of the modern acrylic ones. These are assembled in felt lined frames and cradles and as much of the plumbing as possible should be carried out before the bath is moved into position, so that only the coupling then has to be done.

Care must be taken when using soldered fittings near these baths. They should be well protected by a flame-proof shield when a blowtorch is used in close proximity.

One of the attractions of the modern bath is that a matching panel can be ordered with the bath to

enhance the design of the new scheme of decoration, and this is a great step forward from the more traditional hardboard faced panel applied to a timber frame.

Baths have the habit of settling after they have been installed and used a few times, leaving an ugly gap around the top edges. This is usually more apparent when the bath has been levelled on blocks of softwood.

These gaps can be tackled in various ways. A mastic sealant can be used in a colour, which matches the bath or surrounding tiles, or the gap can be covered with quadrant ceramic tiles. Alternatively new tiles can be applied onto the old and brought down to the bath top level.

Think about these options carefully before you proceed with plans to update an existing bathroom. Even if you do not intend to carry out the work yourself, discuss it in detail with your contractor so that there can be no doubt about what your final requirements will be.

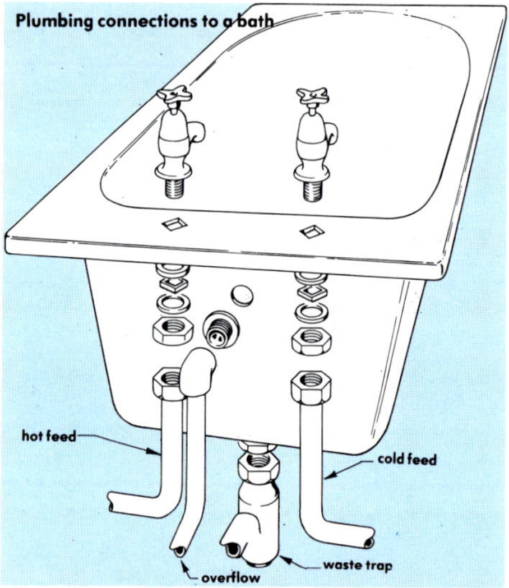

Bidets

Regulations concerning the installation of a bidet depend on the type being used. The simplest 'over the rim' supply fills the bowl from the rim with mixed hot and cold water. Usually this can be plumbed in from the existing supplies feeding bath and basin.

The more sophisticated bidet also has a rim supply of mixed hot and cold water which warms the seat and can be diverted into an ascending spray from a rose sited in the base of the bowl. It is this latter facility which calls for separate supply pipes from the cold water storage tank and hot water cylinder. This precaution is required simply to prevent contaminated water in the bowl being siphoned back into the water supply.

The cold feed should be taken from the same level at the storage tank as the other cold feed supply pipe and it should be controlled by its own gate valve soon after leaving the tank. The inlet to the bidet should be at least 2.75m/9ft below the base of the cold water storage tank. The hot feed should be taken from a tee fitting in the vent pipe just above where it joins the hot water supply pipe at the top of the cylinder.

The waste outlet from a bidet is connected through a trap and discharged in exactly the same way as a bath, basin or sink waste.

The bidet has become accepted as an essential part of the modern bathroom. It is an important functional accessory to health and hygiene.

Shower Units

There is an ever increasing demand for showers in the home and the reason for this is not difficult to understand. Certainly the speed with which a shower can be taken and the saving that can be made on bills are two important considerations which have led to this rise in demand. Needless to say the choice of units available on the market is bewildering.

We have certainly come a long way since the days when a shower consisted of pushing a rubber hose onto the bath taps to provide a rinsing spray.

Nowadays these rather inadequate fittings have given way to the bath and shower mixer unit, where a lever button diverts the water from the bath filling to the shower spray.

The unit is the simplest of all shower controls to fit, as it connects directly onto the hot and cold feed pipes supplying the bath taps. The only requirement for an effective shower is that a distance of 915mm/3ft exists between the bottom of the cold storage tank and the highest extension point of the handset.

But the ever-growing demand is for a separate shower unit which can be housed in the bathroom or somewhere else in the house. Having decided where your shower should be installed you are then faced with the choice of unit to use.

Here the Mira book *A Shower in Your Home* is recommended. Produced by Walker Crosweller & Co Ltd of Cheltenham, Glos, renowned for the quality of their shower fittings, it covers every conceivable aspect of shower selection and installation. Broadly speaking, if you can put a tank in the loft then the answer is to go for a mixer shower. If you cannot, one solution is to go for the instant electric shower.

Instant showers

These have flooded onto the market in recent years and the quality varies a great deal. The flow from an instant shower will not be as great as that from a mixer-type shower, even when a 7Kw heater is incorporated. A quality unit which incorporates a 'temperature stabilizer' will even out the flow of water through it, so that even if the mains inlet pressure varies, the shower temperature will not change dramatically. As a general rule the flow will reduce as you increase the temperature requirement, and this will be more apparent in the winter months when the mains temperature is at its lowest.

They must be wired in accordance with IEE regulations, connected to a suitably rated independent fused electricity supply with a separate on/off switch. In a bathroom this must be a ceiling mounted double pole pullcord switch. It is essential that this work is carried out by a qualified contractor.

Certain multipoint gas water heaters can be used to run a mixer-type shower. This is worth considering if you have a suitable gas heater already installed in a bathroom or kitchen within a reasonable distance of the proposed shower site.

Installed mixer showers

If you have an existing efficient stored system of hot and cold water, a mixer shower will provide the most economic supply of hot water, delivering nearly twice as much volume of water as an instant electric unit at considerably less cost.

Two separate controls will regulate the temperature of the mix and the force of the spray. In an ideal situation the pressure from both hot and cold feeds should be the same, and this is usually the case in most households. The cold feed should be supplied by a separate pipe running direct from the storage tank to the shower unit.

The force of the shower spray depends on the available head of water – that is the distance between the spray outlet and the base of the storage tank above. The minimum requirement is 195mm/3ft, and any increase in this distance will proportionately increase the force of the spray. If a minimum distance cannot be achieved for lack of height, adequate shower facilities can still be provided by the installation of a pump.

Thermostatic valves

This type of valve is the ultimate in shower installations. It is operated by two controls in the same way governing the flow and the temperature.

The built-in thermostat in this type of unit guarantees the pre-selected temperature regardless of any change in pressure in the supply. This means that both hot and cold feeds can be taken as branches from existing pipe runs if necessary. The most important advantage is that an upper temperature can be set as a safeguard against scalding which is a key factor where children and old people are concerned.

The bath is an ideal place over which to install a shower where space is otherwise limited. A shower curtain is the cheapest form of enclosure although various screen enclosures are available. There is even a shower screen roller blind on the market for use with bath showers called Aquanova.

A separate shower cubicle has its advantages as it can be fully enclosed and provides additional bathing facilities in the house. Remember though that once outside the confines of the bath, a separate waste outlet to the drain complete with trap will be required. It is important to leave access to this trap under the shower just in case a blockage occurs. This may mean building up the base on a platform. Base trays are available in a variety of finishes including plastic, steel or glazed fireclay. Where restricted space prevents the use of a standard size tray, a base can be formed from ceramic tiles to good effect.

There are many possible alternatives to a bathroom where a shower unit can be installed. Room can often be found in a bedroom, on a landing or even in an old style pantry if some alteration is contemplated to the kitchen layout. Remember that your main requirements for siting a shower are an adequate supply of hot and cold water, a minimum head of water of 195mm/3ft, and a convenient waste outlet to drainage.

It might be that you qualify for a grant if your present bathroom facilities are inadequate or you have to provide for an elderly or disabled relative.

So before going ahead with an installation contact your local authority first for advice on a grant.

If a shower enclosure makes use of existing wall surfaces or if separate partitions are to be erected, it is important to provide waterproof finishes for the job such as ceramic tiles or plastic laminate. This is vital if moisture is to be prevented from creeping into adjoining areas.

Condensation can be greatly increased in a bedroom if an open shower is installed. A completely enclosed cabinet however will enable the shower to be used and drained behind closed doors and then opened for ventilation when dry. Always place the spray control on a side wall and never the back wall. This ensures the shower can be turned on from the outside without getting an arm soaked.

You may be plagued with periodic growths of mould in your shower, particularly in autumn. Treat this with an application of household bleach solution used in well-ventilated conditions.

Installing a New Tank

The cold water storage tank is the central supply point for all the plumbing in the house except for the rising main. It also carries a large volume of water above your head, consequently it should be inspected periodically to see whether it is in good condition.

In the old galvanized tanks, corrosion is the main cause for concern. This usually starts in the bottom as a thick red sludge and gradually eats its way through the metal until a hole appears. The first signs of trouble may be a small stain on the ceiling beneath due to a very slow drip. Before a tank gets to that condition, its life can be extended by suspending a sacrificial anode into the water. This lump of magnesium has a higher electrical potential than zinc. The electrolytic action between the zinc and the magnesium causes the anode to dissolve to the benefit of the tank metal, thus prolonging its life.

When changing an old tank for a new plastic or glass-fibre replacement, all the water will have to be drained away and the rising main supply shut off. Once a tank is disconnected it can prove a nuisance if left in the loft space. An old tank can be cut into four with a general purpose saw and easily passed through the loft opening to the floor below. After the appropriate holes have been cut in the new tank the pipework can be reconnected. It may have to be extended or slightly adapted in places. Most modern tanks have sloping sides, whether

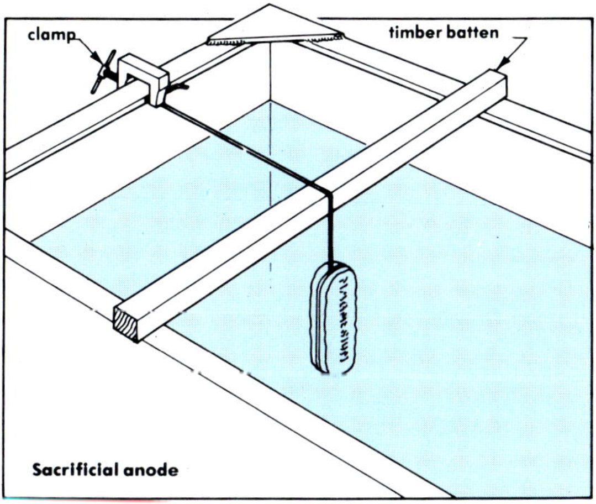

Sacrificial anode

Stages of corrosion in a galvanized metal tank

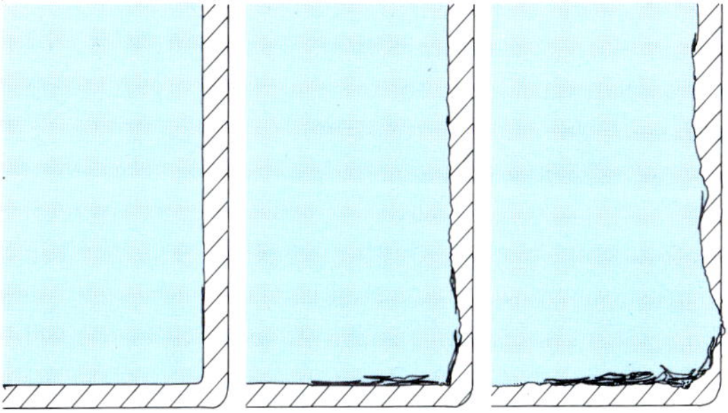

they are circular or rectangular in shape. It is essential to see that the pipework is connected squarely to the sides which may mean altering the angle of the pipe. Failure to do this might lead to strain being put on the tank as the nuts are tightened causing splitting to occur.

Fitting Washing Machines and Dishwashers

One of the most common plumbing jobs to be done in a kitchen is the fitting of a washing machine or dishwasher. This entails extending an existing hot and cold supply to the appliance and running a waste pipe away from it to an outside gully.

The usual method is to insert tee connections into the two supply pipes and fix stopcocks at the end of short extension pipes to which the flexible hoses of the machine are coupled. Often this will mean that one of the extension pipes has to be bent to clear the other supply pipe. There is a useful flexible copper fitting available which makes this job simple to carry out. Kontite thru-valves can also be used to provide the extension supply of hot and cold water to the machine. These are fitted into the existing supplies in place of tee connections. The flexible hoses can then be connected directly to the ends of the valves.

Another method of obtaining a feed is to fit an Opella plumbing-in kit, where the stopcock is fixed directly onto the supply pipe without the need to cut it. To fit the Opella, turn off the water supply and drill an 8mm/$\frac{5}{16}$in hole through the front wall of the pipe only. Then the body of the tap is clamped to it in two sections. As a further development of this type of fitting, Mr Plumber Ltd has manufactured a self-boring version for direct connection to the flexible hose. It is an extremely quick method of providing a supply of water for appliances in the kitchen.

The outlet hose of the appliance will allow water to be discharged over the kitchen sink but it is far more convenient to fit this permanently into its own waste outlet pipe complete with a trap to be discharged over a gully outside. Mr Plumber Ltd has also introduced a plumbing-out set which can be connected to an existing waste outlet without the need to cut through the waste pipe. A self boring tool supplied with the fitting will form an aperture to house the outlet hose coupling which is clamped into place.

Waste Outlets and Overflows

A waste fitting in a bath, basin or sink may start to leak with the tell-tale drip marks appearing on the floor beneath. This can result from a breakdown in the mastic joint or a badly worn washer. To cure the problem the waste fitting will have to be taken out.

First disconnect the trap, so that the backnut holding the waste in position can be loosened and removed. Often the complete waste will turn with the spanner and it will be necessary to grip the grating with pliers to break the joint. Once it is apart, clean away any old traces of putty and set it back on a bed of fresh putty replacing the washer if necessary.

Overflows to baths, basins and sinks have a nasty habit of not carrying the water away as quickly as it enters when taps are in full flow. Flooding often results from this design deficiency but the problem can be made worse by a waste outlet being fitted incorrectly. The slots in the waste between the grating and the threaded tail must line up with the outlet of the overflow pipe or channel. Test your waste overflows to see whether they carry excess water away efficiently to prevent flooding.

Removing a waste

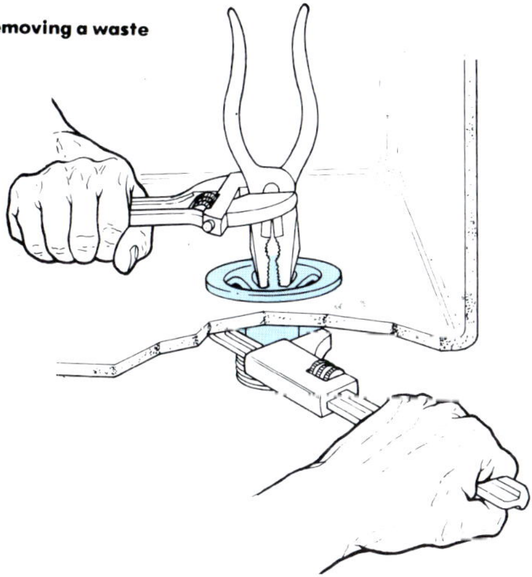

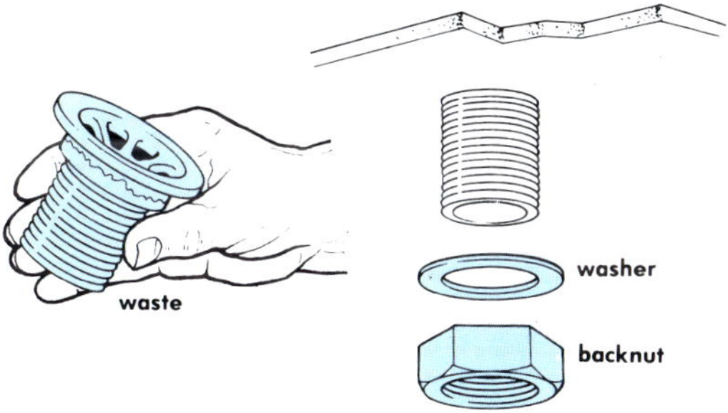

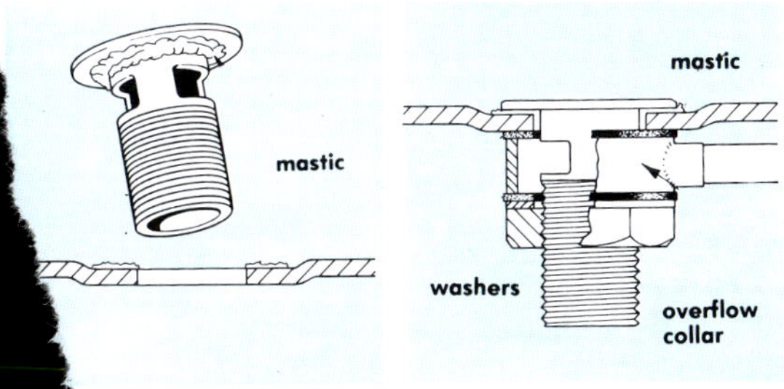

Waste Disposal Units

A waste disposal unit is a practical asset in a kitchen and considerably reduces the amount of disposable rubbish to be collected at the end of each week.

For most disposal units a sink outlet hole of 89mm/3½in diameter within and concentric to a

114mm/$4\frac{1}{2}$in diameter recess is required. New sink tops are available pre-cut to these dimensions by the supplier so that fitting becomes a very straightforward operation when a kitchen is being installed.

Where fitting has to be carried out to an existing stainless steel sink with a standard undersize outlet hole, this can be enlarged by using a sink modification kit, which is readily available from the manufacturer of the waste disposal unit. The modification is carried out in two stages. First the existing hole is enlarged using a special saw frame, then the surrounding recess is formed with a tool which consists of a centre pin and two mating parts – a punch and a die. These two parts are drawn up

together by means of six allen screws which are steadily tightened in sequence.

With the recess accurately formed the sink suspension unit can be clamped into place. The disposer unit is then hung beneath, usually with a quick release assembly to facilitate easy servicing.

An elbow and 38mm/1½in diameter waste outlet pipe should be used with a P- or S-trap. A bottle trap should not be used as it is not suitable for this type of unit. It is essential to have no sharp bends in the pipe run from the disposer to the gully and the discharge end of the pipe should be set below the grid of the gully to prevent a build-up of waste which would lead to an overflow.

A property without main drainage is not precluded from using a waste disposal unit. A septic tank of 3640 litres/800 gallons in good working order is perfectly adequate to accommodate the output.

The unit must be wired to a double pole fused spur switch with the correct fuse rating and be properly earthed. The method of activating a disposer unit varies with different models but the latest Tweeny 125 relies on modern technology.

A self-reversing activator switch is pneumatically operated without any electrical connectors to the unit itself. A button controls the on/off and reverse spin of the cutter blades and the fibre optic light guide indicates whether the motor is running, overloaded or in the on or the off position.

Once installed a waste disposal unit does not require routine maintenance and usually when servicing is necessary, it can be carried out on the spot by a servicing agent. It should always be run with an adequate flow of water passing through it to flush the ground waste from the chamber. Gardening enthusiasts with a liking for natural compost can utilize the strained shreddings from the disposal unit for recycling as fertilizer.

Softened Water

It is ironic that the subject of plumbing concerns the carrying of water to and about our homes and yet the type of water which it brings is seldom given a second thought. In the UK approximately 65 per cent of our homes suffer from hard water, the degree of hardness being created by the chalk and limestone which remain dissolved within it.

If you live in a hard water area, you will see the scale and fur which forms in your kettle but most problems occur within the pipework, the taps and appliances which are largely hidden from view. Heating elements are particularly prone to accumulating scale, which results in a loss of efficiency. It only requires about 3mm/$\frac{1}{8}$in of scale to build up on an immersion heater for example, to reduce its heating efficiency by almost 15 per cent. The reaction of hard water with soap causes a grease-like scum to form which is difficult to remove from the skin and fabrics and can be clearly seen deposited around a basin or bath after use.

A water softener removes this hardness in the following way. The main supply of water is diverted through a pressure cylinder which contains a special resin. The resin substitutes soft sodium for dissolved calcium and other hard minerals.

By softening the water, the resin is depleted of sodium and is regenerated by rinsing with a brine solution to carry away the hard minerals and replace more sodium.

The process continues indefinitely and is fully automated, the number of rinsings each week being dependent on the volume of domestic water consumed. A small amount of granular salt has to be introduced into the base of the unit from time to time to keep the brine solution at full strength.

Installation is straightforward once you have decided on the model to suit your requirements. The main supply is diverted through the softener in a loop by means of two compression tee fittings with a stopcock either side of the unit. If you wish to retain hard water for drinking purposes then the loop should be taken from the rising main after it branches from the kitchen tap and garden tap supplies. Certainly it would be wasteful to run a softened supply to the outside tap. The only other requirement will be drainage pipes to an outside gully for the rinsing process and a safety overflow pipe, neither of which will require traps.

Modern softeners are not unattractive and can be left free standing or placed in a cupboard. A fully automatic time-controlled water softener will require an independently fused electric supply to the time clock within the unit. If this type of unit is left for a period of time, it will be necessary to turn off the supply to the time clock to prevent the automatic regeneration of the cylinder when this is not required. Recent developments in automatic regeneration have resulted in the Kinetic softener which does not require electricity. It contains a control valve which meters the water and alternates the regeneration between two separate cylinders, giving an uninterrupted supply of soft water.

The modest running cost of a softener is offset by the greatly reduced demand for soap and washing powder, quite apart from the longer running life of plumbing and appliances alike. Softened water will slowly erode any build up of scale which has been deposited by hard water in the past. It will be

very noticeable if a softened supply suddenly reverts to hardness without warning. If this occurs, it usually indicates that the salt needs replenishing.

Central Heating

Central heating certainly falls within the sphere of plumbing but it is such a wide subject that it can only be touched upon in this book. The installation of a system is a time-consuming job but it is not beyond the capabilities of anyone who has a working knowledge of how to put pipework together.

The success of a good central heating system depends very much on the quality of the design of a layout and here you require the services of an expert in the subject. In addition to the type of boiler required the design must cover the entire layout of the house, room by room, to provide an even temperature throughout a dwelling at the most economic running cost. The electrical wiring of a fully automated system is often fairly complex and needs to be installed by a qualified person.

Finally when a system is running well, it must be serviced regularly to keep it in good working order. Thermostats, time clocks, valves and pumps tend to be reliable and just need checking periodically to see that they are running correctly. The boiler on the other hand requires regular maintenance. A burner must be clean and correctly set to burn the right mix of air and fuel to be efficient.

Swimming Pools

A swimming pool installation is the one remaining area where there is a plumbing requirement. Like central heating it is a subject which can only be lightly touched upon in this book as both construction and maintenance can involve a wide range of materials, finishes and techniques which are too extensive to mention.

There are certain local authority and water authority regulations to comply with and as these regulations are constantly under review, it is well worth contacting the Swimming Pool and Allied Trades Association (SPATA) for current information on the subject before you go ahead with any plans to install a pool of your own.

The successful running of a pool depends upon the efficient circulation of water in a continuous loop during which it is cleaned, disinfected nd heated. In this sequence of events it is carefully balanced after filling, so that the water level only needs to be topped up to replenish the volume lost through evaporation and the periodic backwashing to the drains, which takes place every time the filtration system needs regenerating. Water is cleaned of debris such as leaves, pollen and dust by circulating through a coarse strainer and then the filtration unit, before returning back to the pool again.

Mechanical cleaning of the water is not sufficient to keep a pool in healthy working condition. The chemical balance has to be controlled by introduc-

ing additives by hand or automatically. Chlorination is the most common and economic method of maintaining the required level of disinfection. A daily test will confirm whether the balance is correct. A test will also check the pH level of the pool – that is the degree of acidity or alkalinity.

An ideal level for pH is 7.5. A lower reading indicates acidity which should be neutralized by the addition of sodium bicarbonate, while a high pH is indicative of excessive alkalinity which should be lowered by the introduction of sodium bisulphate. All pool chemicals should be handled with the greatest care and used strictly in accordance with the manufacturers' instructions.

Finally there must be facilities available to heat the water if maximum use is to be made of a swimming pool in our temperate climate. Choosing a system can be difficult and you would be wise to take considerable advice before making a decision.

Certainly where solar heating is concerned, after the initial expense, energy will be free and readily available for heating pool water when it is required. Plastic pipes and fittings are used almost entirely where swimming pools are concerned and these should be adequately protected by burial underground or with adequate supports above ground. Rigid uPVC pipes should be solvent welded and flexible alkathene used with compression fittings.

Pumps heaters and lighting must be wired into the system by a qualified electrical contractor and once installed, regularly maintained. Remember that electricity and water form a lethal combination in the wrong hands.

Summary

Now that you have a greater understanding of how the plumbing in your home works, you will be in a better position to face any problems which might occur in the course of the day-to-day functioning of a service, which is on tap 24 hours a day for the overwhelming majority of the community. Moreover now that you are aware of the very worst things that can go wrong with the water supply and drainage, you will be better equipped to put things right for yourself or better still, take sufficient precautions to prevent them happening in the first place.

If as a result you manage to do one or two practical jobs successfully in the home so much the better. One thing is certain, time is usually on the side of the DIY operative and where plumbing is concerned this means that with a little care and patience, pipework can be taken where you want it to go. So often it is run the shortest possible distance between two points with very ugly results. Like most other jobs in the home, a successful conclusion is invariably reached by planning it out before you start thus deriving some degree of satisfaction from completing the work yourself.